Inspired by
John Muir

*A Guide to Studying Nature,
Capturing Our Stories &
Advocating for Wild Places*

By Janice Kelley

About the Book
Inspired by John Muir is one in a series of products within the Nature Detectives outdoor experience program. To order additional copies, learn more about Nature Detectives programs, activities and resources, visit https://naturedetectivesusa.com.

Additional books by the author in the series
What Song does the Rain Sing?
Nature Detectives Leader Training Guide

Additional books by the author
Mornings on Fair Oaks Bridge, Watching Wildlife on the Lower American River
In Nature's time

Copyright 2020. Janice Kelley. All rights reserved. No part of this publication may be reproduced, distributed or transmitted in any form or by any means, without prior written permission of the author. Contact Janice at outdoorjan@att.net.

Inspired by John Muir/Janice Kelley. -- 1st ed.
ISBN 978-0-9715467-7-6

Excerpted and revised from Through the Eyes of John Muir, Practices in Environmental Stewardship by Janice Kelley

Dedication

To the children who will keep the essence of John Muir close to their heart; and bring forward his wisdom, determination and enthusiasm for preserving wild places and wild things for future generations to enjoy.

"In every walk with Nature, one receives far more than he seeks. All creation is connected, beautiful and whole."

John Muir

Contents

Part One – John Muir Life and Accomplishments 9
Life at a Glance 11
Child and Young Adult 13
Naturalist, Adventurer and Writer 15
Life at Martinez Ranch 17
A Lifetime of Activism 19
Strentzel-Muir Ranch 21
John Muir Timeline 22

Part Two – Actions & Activities 23
The John Muir Story 25
    John Muir Biography Questions 25
    Personal Reflections 26
    Who is John Muir? Crossword Puzzle 30
    John Muir: The Scientist Crossword Puzzle 31
    Story of John Muir 32
    1880s Child: What do you have in common? 33
    John Muir Quotations Reflection Project 34

Our Stories & Storytelling 37
    Building Storytelling Skills 38
    Decision Map 39
    Who Am I? 40
    Family Stories 41
    Other People, Other Places 42
    Our Changing Community 43

Wonders of Nature 44
    Naturalist Skills 45
    Discovery Journal 46
    Sample Journal Page 47
    Journal Questions 48
    Searching for Evidence 49
    Listen Deeply and Watch Closely 50

Habitat High Rise	51
Meet a Tree	52
Explore a Special Place	53
"What am I?"	54

Advocacy 57
    Modern Day John Muir 58
    Advocacy Project 59
    Role of Resource Agencies 60
    Vision for the Future 62

Part Three – Appendix 65
Story Answer Sheet 66
Biography Answer Sheet 67
Who is John Muir? Crossword answers 69
John Muir: Scientist Crossword answers 70
Who Am I? Answers 71
Books About John Muir 71
Glossary 72
Bibliography 75

Introduction

This book consists of three sections inspired by John Muir's life, practices and accomplishments: The first part is a series of short descriptions that highlight parts of John Muir's life and accomplishments. He spent a lifetime working to preserve wilderness areas, forests, mountains, rivers and meadows, so wildlife can thrive. He wanted to preserve beautiful places so we can feel a meaningful connection with the natural world, and nourish our bodies, hearts and minds at the same time. So we can observe nature in awe and wonder, listen to the music of the wind, the voices the trees and the sounds of birds and other wildlife as they engage in their daily rituals across landscapes and skies. By reading Muir's thoughts about how he sees the world, you learn his values and what he believed was most important about the natural world.

The second section is a series of actions, questions, and activities to reflect on Muir's life and inspire thinking about how you relate to the places you live, your family stories and your community. *Wonders of Nature* presents opportunities to *listen deeply and watch closely*, become a skilled nature observer, and record experiences in your nature journal. This is your invitation to consider "how you think," in addition to "facts to think about." *Advocacy* presents examples how you can get involved in local issues that concern you and be part of a solution.

As we grow and find our way in our community, we can all benefit from having helpers and guides. These people show us a way through challenges and help us solve problems. By learning about John Muir, you can hold his lifetime practices as a role model for making a difference in your community. He represents individuals around the world – in history and contemporary times - who struggle and persevere to make the world a better place where anyone can thrive.

The third section is the Appendix at the back of the book includes answers to all activities and a glossary. This book scratches the surface of what there is to know about John Muir's life. A list of other books about him and a bibliography citing the sources used to create Muir's profile are also in the Appendix.

Part One

Life and Accomplishments

John Muir's Home

Sitting in his Scribble Den

John Muir and Teddy Roosevelt In Yosemite

Walking through Yosemite

John Muir at a Glance

JOHN MUIR is often remembered around the world as a writer, speaker, teacher, scientist, naturalist, botanist, storyteller, guide, rancher and adventurer.

He defined and later led the American conservation movement, established and became the first president of the Sierra Club, and was recognized as the father of America's national parks. Muir was also a prolific inventor. His influence on two American presidents led to establishing seven national parks, 23 monuments and preserving millions of acres of forested land.

Leading by example, Muir's influence shaped the way people around the world experience the outdoors and wilderness areas of the United States.

Muir is often regarded as the "son of the wilderness." This image of Muir speaks to the second of three stages in his life: the first as a child through young adulthood; the second as an explorer and naturalist; and the third, his final years as a successful Martinez fruit rancher, conservationist and father. Muir's childhood and young adult experiences set the foundation for decisions and beliefs in his later years.

The John Muir National Historic Site, Muir Woods National Monument, Muir Glacier in Glacier Bay National Park, John Muir Trail, many wilderness areas, the California state quarter, two US postage stamps, schools, hospitals and numerous other places were named to celebrate the life an accomplishments of John Muir.

His quotations are written in books and posted to websites; displayed on banners that hang in national park visitor centers; and spoken in videos about Muir's life, national parks, wild lands and stories of the environment. His enduring legacy of environmental stewardship remains strong more than 100 years after his death.

Yet, this brief description represents only a fraction of his life. Muir was a man of many talents, trades and interests. Muir was especially skilled at influencing the influencers - his relationship with President Theodore Roosevelt led to the preservation of millions of acres of forest and wild lands.

Muir lived the last year of his life with his wife Louise and their daughters Helen and Wanda on a large fruit ranch in Martinez, California. The ranch is located about 35 miles northeast of San Francisco. He wrote many persuasive essays in his "Scribble Den" at home. Using the ranch has his home base, he traveled around the world to research, explore and speak while he lived at the ranch. Muir wrote more than 10 books and hundreds of articles. He left the ranch from July to October before the work of the annual fruit harvest began.

Profits from sales and leases of parts of the Strentzel-Muir Ranch made it possible for him to support his family and leave home to become an environmental champion.

Child to Young Adult

From a very young age, John Muir was curious about nature and felt at home in wild places. Muir found joy in the natural beauty of the outdoors. He treasured the creatures and the forces of nature that shaped the world as he knew it. Young Muir did not know at the time that this curiosity and love of nature would become the guiding principles that led to his becoming internationally recognized as the founder of the American conservation movement and numerous other roles.

"When I was a boy in Scotland, I was fond of everything that was wild and all my life I've been growing fonder and fonder of wild places and wild creatures ... Oh, the blessed enchantment of those Saturday runaways in the prime of spring!"

John Muir was born April 21, 1838. He had two brothers and four sisters. Beginning in his youngest days on the family's farm, Muir would run to the seashore or pastures to hear birds sing and search for their nests. He enjoyed studying wildlife, exploring tide pools and climbed the ruins of the Dunbar Castle.

In 1849, the family immigrated to Wisconsin and established Fountain Lake Farm. Muir had already studied the American wilderness while living in Scotland and was fascinated by it. He read books about land that had never been changed by man, trees that grew so tall because they had not been cut, and the earth not plowed. He was anxious to discover the treasures of the wilderness.

Muir the Inventor

His first invention was a full-scale model of a self-setting sawmill. Without a proper workshop, Muir whittled his own tools from wood. Soon he had developed water wheels, door locks and latches, thermometers, a barometer, a series of clocks, a lamp lighter, a fire lighter and other mechanical devices. All Muir's devices were whittled out of scraps of woods and fastened together with pegs and rope.

He invented a series of clocks. These were large, complex and freestanding devices using a series of cogs, wheels and levers. Muir designed them based on how he thought a clock should operate. The family had no clocks in the house and he never saw the inner workings of a clock. Muir called these clocks his "early rising machine." They featured special moving parts that would light fires and a lamp. Each clock was specially made so it would tip a part of his bed to get him out of it in the morning.

Muir believed that entering the state fair was the first step to advancing his career goals of securing a job either in a factory as an engineer, or in medicine. His inventions were the most popular displays at the fair, attracting huge crowds and a front-page feature story in the following day's newspaper. Visitors crowded into the exhibit hall to see his grand inventions. He was awarded a prize of $15.

While attending the state fair he met Jeanne Carr, wife of Professor Ezra Carr at University of Wisconsin. She encouraged him to apply for enrollment in the university. From that day forward, Jeanne became his lifelong mentor. Muir entered the University of Wisconsin in 1861, the same year the Civil War began.

Canada Experience

Muir left school and traveled to Canada during the Civil War. With his knowledge of science, Muir observed the rugged valleys and understood how they had been formed over the earth's long geologic history. "Nature, he realized, was written in hieroglyphics that science could help him read, decipher, and appreciate in new ways."

He returned to America after the Civil War ended and eventually found work at a carriage factory in Indiana. In spite of his talents for inventions and working with machinery, Muir feared he had become "a wandering star, with no fixed object or trajectory."

In March of 1867, Muir was 29 years old. He was adjusting a machine when a file he held in his hand slipped and pierced the cornea of his right eye. Within hours he lost sight in both eyes.

Naturalist, Adventurer and Writer

After Muir recovered his eyesight many weeks later, he decided to take a long walk and explore the wilderness on his own. He prepared for this 1,000-mile walk through the southern region of the United States by inscribing in his journal, "John Muir, Earth-planet, Universe."

This new address was his way of saying that he had cut ties to any specific place and now belonged only to the planet. His journey was a rebellion against middle-class conventions, "searching for a sense of belonging, a meaningful occupation and humanity's place in the natural world." He wrote daily in his journal to describe the people, places, and his experiences. Muir walked through the region, staying with locals who generously offered him a place to sleep and food to eat.

Muir traveled to Cuba. Within one month he could no longer stand the weather. Muir found an ad in a New York newspaper that featured a ship sailing to California and promised cheap fares. He expected that the cooler forests and mountains would improve his health.

In March of 1868, Muir passed under the Golden Gate Bridge. When he exited the ship, Muir saw only the commercial buildings of San Francisco. He met a workman at the waterfront and asked for directions to leave town. The man replied, "Where do you want to go?" Muir responded, "Anywhere that is wild." From that moment, Muir began his walk along the Coastal Range and then inward bound on his way to Yosemite Valley.

Muir discovered that he found a home in California. He could start his life anew. It suit him body and soul. Although he did not know it when he arrived, California was the only place he would ever live for the rest of his life. Years later Muir wrote in an 1898 issue of *Atlantic Monthly*,

> "Climb the mountains and get their good tidings. Nature's peace will flow into you as sunshine flows into trees. The winds will blow their own freshness into you, and the storms their energy, while cares will drop off like autumn leaves"

Yosemite Wilderness

"Muir entered Yosemite at a pivotal moment, when far reaching decisions were being made about its future, and indeed about the future of the American West and how to preserve its wonderful natural assets from unregulated self-interest." Muir took little interest in the political side of the issue at the time. (Worster, 2008)

When Muir was in Yosemite, he discovered that the Yosemite Valley was not carved by erosion from the Merced River, as theorized at that time by the scientific community. The valley was actually carved and polished by glaciers. He reached his conclusions by carefully observing the rocks, cliffs, ridges and domes of the Sierra. As proof of glacial movement, he placed sticks into the ice and stretched a fish line across them. Then Muir measured movement of the sticks.

> "Wildness is a necessity; and that mountain parks and reservations are useful not only as fountains of timber and irrigating rivers, but as fountains of life."

In the Overland Monthly magazines of San Francisco magazine, his first series of articles appeared in 1871. His first series of articles on the findings of his research on glaciers appeared under a common title, "Studies in the Sierra." He continued writing persuasive stories for tourists, advising them to "escape the bonds of urban labor by experiencing the refreshment of the mountains."

Muir stayed in the Sierra during bitter rain, cold and winds. He climbed to the top of a Douglas spruce to find out how trees behaved in a wild storm. One author wrote, "The tree beneath him rocked and swirled, forward, backward, around and round. No bucking mustang ever gave him such a ride." Muir often said,

> "The power of imagination makes us infinite."

From his position in the tree, Muir describes hearing in the winds the roar of the seas they had passed over, and breathed a thousand fragrances released from deep pine forest.

Life at Martinez Ranch

Louise encouraged him to travel because he was so weakened by the labors of the ranch. "I am all nerve shaken and lean as a crow - loaded with care, work and worry," he wrote in a letter to one of his brothers. She understood he needed time "to climb the peaks, sleep in alpine meadows and write books about the glories of what he saw and heard." His periodic trips to Alaska, Yosemite and other parts around the nation and the world energized him. One trip to Alaska he travels with *Stickeen* – a small dog who inspired another of Muir's adventure stories.

His two daughters, Wanda and Helen, spent their childhood playing with an assortment of animals the family kept on the farm, including turkeys and guinea pigs. He took his daughters on walks up the hills of the ranch pointing out every flower bloom with delight and calling them by name.

Under Dr. Strentzel's supervision, the ranch grew a wide assortment of fruits and nuts including apples, cherries, figs, olives, oranges, pears, peaches, pecans, plum, pomegranate, quince, raisins and strawberries. By 1890, Muir planted two-thirds of the ranch as vineyards with six varieties of grapes. Another part of the ranch was dedicated to cattle grazing and growing hay and grains.

Also by this time, ranchers produced fewer varieties of fruit to increase productivity. Muir, a smart businessman, chose to grow the fruits that were the most profitable. He applied his talent for inventing things to improve ranch operations. Muir invented a machine that helped ranch workers plant vines in a straight line.

The days when Muir ventured into the wilderness, he enjoyed the sweet sounds of birds. However, when he caught birds landing on his fruit trees, he called them a nuisance because they ate his fruit. Muir was very specific about his farming practices to maximize his resources. He never used poison on his trees and planted hillsides with vineyards to avoid erosion. He also convinced the railroad company to build a station at the edge of his ranch to make it faster and easier to ship his produce to market.

Muir had been steadily selling and leasing large chunks of the ranch for years. He used the money to support his family and provide the funding he needed to travel and write. In 1891, Muir immersed himself full time into his conservation work and writing. He passed the ranch management to his son-in-law Tom Hanna, who married Muir's eldest daughter Wanda. The Hannas continued to subdivide the ranch, although most of the lands were still being farmed. The Hanna's sold all their properties, except the family cemetery by 1919, five years after Muir's death. The ranch was purchased many years later by the National Park Service and renamed the John Muir National Historic Site.

Muir's commented during his battle to save Hetch Hetchy Valley.

In an 1896 article in the Sierra Club Bulletin, he wrote, "The battle we have fought, and are still fighting ... is a part of the eternal conflict between right and wrong, and we cannot expect to see an end of it."

A Lifetime of Activism

The final years of Muir's life was when he saw the impact of his lifetime of public service. Muir had been a catalyst to turn public concerns into meaningful actions. Highlighted below are selections of his most important adventures, battles and accomplishments.

He became a self-described "tramp" because he wanted to grow in the heart of nature and be true to his own instincts. Once he entered the wilderness and learned of its beauty, power and healing qualities, he felt compelled to share its value with others. It was Muir's total immersion in the beauty of nature that fueled his appreciation of the natural world and, in turn, led to his life's work.

- Camped out privately with President Theodore Roosevelt so they could experience the majesty of the park together. Muir used the camping trip to influence President Roosevelt's decision to create Yosemite as a national park.

- His influence on Roosevelt led to the establishment of five national parks, 23 national monuments and 148 million acres of national forest

- Joined a US Forest Commission team in 1896 to survey forests and timberlands of the West Coast and Southwest. Findings in the report inspired President Cleveland to make changes in timber and mining laws.

- Influenced President Cleveland to set aside an additional 21 million acres of land for preservation, 13 new reservations and two new national parks (Grand Canyon in Arizona and Mt. Rainier in Washington state) in addition to lands already set aside by President Theodore Roosevelt.

- Became actively involved in the preservation of the Giant Sequoias in Sequoia and General Grant (later renamed to Kings Canyon) National Parks. Muir published the book, Our National Parks by combining all the articles he had written for the Atlantic Monthly into one volume.

- A law passed two years after this death that placed all national parks under one director who was empowered to "conserve the scenery and the natural and historic objects and wildlife in the parks." John Muir is considered to be the father of the national park system.

Battle for Hetch Hetchy

Muir's decade long quest to save Hetch Hetchy Valley was his final battle and crushing defeat. The fight continued for more than 10 years. It enlisted support of two consecutive presidents, assorted senators, prominent business leaders, newspaper publishers and many others. He believed the Sierra Club (based in San Francisco) failed him and never forgave them for their absence of support. The campaign to Restore Hetch Hetchy Valley remains active.

> *"That anyone would try to destroy such a place seems incredible; but sad experience show that there are people good enough and bad enough for anything"* ("The Hetch Hetchy Valley,") Sierra Club Bulletin, 2008.

Muir believed this battle was a life and death struggle for the preservation of Yosemite National Park. The Hetch Hetchy reservoir was to be a source for water and hydroelectric power for residents of San Francisco hundreds of miles away. When President Wilson was elected president in 1912, he appointed as his Secretary of Interior, Franklin K. Lane - a San Francisco lawyer and advocate for the Hetch Hetchy project. The president signed the bill into law within a few months after his election.

Muir was devastated over the loss. His fight had taken a tremendous toll on his body and soul. He was thin, frail and exhausted. Now living alone on the ranch, since his wife died, Muir decided to visit Helen in Arizona for some relaxation. He packed up his Alaska manuscript and arrived in Arizona during a bitter wind and cold temperatures. Muir caught pneumonia and was taken to a hospital in Los Angeles. He died alone on Christmas Eve 1914. Muir was 76 years old.

Strentzel-Muir Ranch

The ranch today is 8.9 acres, a fraction of the original 2,300-acre ranch owned by John Strentzel. The Muir House is a 10,000 square foot mansion built in 1882 by Dr. and Mrs. Strentzel. The formal Italian Villa design was popular with wealthy homeowners during that era. Dr. Strentzel wanted the house safe from flooding by Franklin Creek, so he built it on the top of a hill. The bell tower on the third floor is 100 feet above the valley floor and provides sweeping views. The bell signaled Muir and his farm workers to return to the house for meals.

The house originally consisted of 14 rooms, a basement, several porches, a full attic, a large kitchen, East and West Parlors and the cupola. Muir added on when he and his wife Louie moved in. The house featured indoor plumbing and a reliable water supply. Phone service was installed 1884. Electricity came in the early 1900s. John Muir and his family moved in after Dr. Strentzel's death in 1890.

The former ranch property became the John Muir National Historic Site in 1964. The goal of the NPS horticulturist is to recreate the property to look as authentic as possible, with fruits planted in their original location.

John Muir Timeline of Life Events

Year Event
1838 Birth
1849 Immigrates to America (Wisconsin)
1860 Enters inventions into the Wisconsin State Fair
1860 Meets Jeanne and Ezra Carr at the university
1861 Enrolls in Wisconsin State University
1867 Machine accident blinds John Muir temporarily
1867 1,000-mile walk
1868 Arrives in Yosemite
1874 Publishes first series of articles "Studies in the Sierra,"
1880 Marries Louise Strentzel
1880 Travels to Alaska with Stickeen
1881 First child is born
1890 Succeeds in his efforts to create Yosemite National Park
1891 Retires from farming and becomes an environmental advocate
1892 Helps form Sierra Club
1903 Camps with President Theodore Roosevelt in Yosemite Valley
1907 Hetch Hetchy Dam fight begins
1914 John Muir dies of pneumonia

For additional information and other timeline dates, visit
https://vault.sierraclub.org/john_muir_exhibit/john_muir_day_study_guide/biographical_timeline.aspx

Part Two

Actions & Activities

John Muir Story

John Muir Biography Questions

Respond to these questions on the blank pages provided.

- What was one of John Muir's first encounters with nature as a young boy?
- Describe one or more of Muir's inventions.
- What was the reason he went on his 1,000-mile walk to the Gulf of Mexico?
- What did Muir discover about how Yosemite was formed?
- What else did Muir do in Yosemite?
- Why was John Muir living on a ranch?
- Describe what motivated Muir to spend his life protecting the wilderness.
- Did John Muir act alone or did he have support to make changes happen? If so, name two people that helped John Muir make changes.
- What were the subjects that Muir wrote about in his articles, books and journals?

Personal Reflection Questions
Respond in your book or in a separate journal.

1. What are important milestones in your life that you can add to a timeline?
2. Give an example of when you have persevered and not given up.
3. Have you or anyone you know invented something new and different?
4. What have you contributed to your family, your school or your community? Do you know other people who have?
5. John Muir enlisted support from other people and relied on mentors. Do you have a source of support or a mentor?
6. What comes to your mind when thinking about the future of the wilderness?
7. Stickeen was a special dog. Muir also developed relationships with squirrels. Do you have a special pet that you take care of and comforts you?

Responses to Questions

Responses to Questions

Responses to Questions

Name _____

Who Was John Muir?

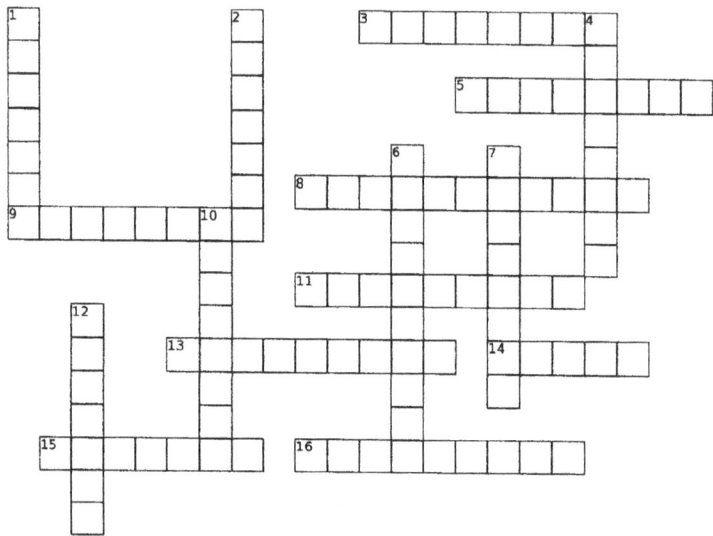

ACROSS

3. Muir had a special talent for building _____.
5. City where he lived and worked on his ranch.
8. The room where he wrote many of his books and stories.
9. One of Muir's favorite animals to watch.
11. What he was called when Muir studied glaciers and created new farming practices.
13. He called the Sierra Nevada _____, the "Range of Light."
14. This is where Muir grew fruits and vegetables to sell.
15. Muir collected and drew hundreds of these.
16. Muir and _____ Roosevelt visited Yosemite valley

DOWN

1. He spent many years surveying these to be sure the trees were healthy.
2. Where he described his adventures, recorded measurements and drew pictures of what he observed.
4. The name of his dog.
6. The special places Muir wanted to preserve.
7. Yosemite Valley was carved from these.
10. A person who studies places no one else has visited.
12. Muir believed logging the forest was a very serious _____.

John Muir: The Scientist

ACROSS

2. John Muir was a _____, because he studied plants, their life, structure, growth and classification.
4. The study of growing flowers, fruits and vegetables in gardens or orchards.
6. The area of science that deals with physical history and structure of the earth, rocks and rock formations is called _____.
10. A steep-sided, U-shaped valley formed by erosion when glaciers move through a river channel.
11. A large mass of ice formed when snow accumulates and stays solid without melting.
12. The physical world we live in, including things, influences and conditions.

DOWN

1. John Muir was called a _____ because he studied nature as a result of direct observation of animals or plants.
2. The area of science that deals with the origin, history, characteristics, life processes and habits of living organisms.
3. John Muir was opposed to this practice of cutting so many trees in the forest that caused long term damage to habitats and stripped the landscape.
5. John Muir founded the _____ movement that involves the careful use of resources to prevent their injury, waste, decay or loss.
7. A geographic area where plants, animals and other organisms, as well as weather and landscape, work together to create life.
8. John Muir was one of the first to apply the area of science that studies the relationships organisms have to each other and the environment.
9. Weather patterns of a specific place that occur over a period of years.

Story of John Muir

Complete the sentences below and fill in using words from the box. Each word can be used one time.

	Key Words	
respect	wandered	observe
treasured	active	exploring
ancient	magnificent	ability
examine	struggle	defend
ambition	reverse	triumph
nation	surveyed	globe
ordeal	opponent	outcome
individuals	journey	solutions

John Muir learned to love and _____ nature when he was a young boy at his family's farm in Scotland. He _____ through fields and forests to _____ the birds, squirrels and other wildlife. Muir always _____ nature. "Climb the mountains and get their good tidings. Nature's peace will flow into you as sunshine flows into the trees."

Muir also had an _____ imagination and a lot of _____ that led to his becoming an inventor. However, Muir could not separate himself from _____ nature for long. He set out on a _____ of 1,000 miles.

A few years later, Muir lived and worked in Yosemite Valley, among the _____ and ancient redwood trees. He took many risks to _____ the rocks in Yosemite to gather scientific evidence that glaciers carved the valley. Muir also climbed trees in wind and rainstorms to discover how they behaved. For more than 25 years, Muir struggled to _____ the forest and wilderness areas. He had the _____ to write persuasive articles so _____ would be interested in finding _____ to preserve wilderness for future generations to enjoy. He worked hard to _____ the damage to forests and habitats as the _____ of too much logging.

One of his many _____ was influencing President Roosevelt to create five national parks. Muir _____ forests around the _____ to help preserve them. Muir's last battle was to prevent the construction of a dam in the Hetch Hetchy Valley. The _____ lasted 10 years and in the end, his _____ won.

The 1880s Child: What do you have in common?

See how you are similar to children who lived in the 1880s. Children played with toys and games. They had their favorite foods too. Place an "X" next to the foods or toys you like, have played with or eaten. Add up the number of "X"s and write the number for each column on the **TOTAL** line at the bottom of the column.

_____	Ice Cream Sundae	_____	Marbles
_____	Hamburger	_____	Chinese Checkers
_____	Pizza	_____	Crayons
_____	Jell-O	_____	Board Games
_____	Chewing Gum	_____	Playing Cards
_____	Peanut Brittle	_____	Jumping Ropes
_____	Milk Chocolate	_____	Toy Trains
_____	Kellogg's Corn Flakes	_____	Rocking Horse
_____	Cream Cheese	_____	Doll
_____	Dr Pepper	_____	Doll Houses
_____	California Oranges	_____	Spinning Tops
_____	Coca Cola	_____	Toy Boats
_____	Frozen vegetables	_____	Pick up Sticks
_____	**TOTAL**	_____	**TOTAL**

John Muir Quotation Reflections

Read through the following series of quotations and choose three or four or more that are the most important or meaningful to you. Outlined are several different methods for additional reflection..

- Draw a picture that illustrates the meaning of the quotation. Write the quotation someone on the picture as a caption.
- Create a collage of words and images that illustrate the meaning.
- Write your impressions in a journal and/or talk with a friend or family about how the quotation changes your thinking about the natural world and our place in it.

Respect for all creatures and creation.

"How narrow we selfish, conceited creatures are in our sympathies? How blind to the rights of all the rest of creation!"

"Killed a rattlesnake that was tranquilly sunning himself in coiled ease about a bunch of grass. After dislodging him by throwing dirt, I killed him by jumping upon him, because no stones or sticks were near. He defended himself bravely, and I ought to have been bitten. He was innocent and deserved life."

"How many mouths Nature has to fill, how may neighbors we have, how little we know about them, and seldom we get in each other's way!"

John Muir's passion and connection to the natural world.

"God himself seems to be always doing his best here, working like a mean in a glow of enthusiasm."

"In every walk with Nature, one receives far more than he seeks." All creation is connected, beautiful and whole.

"The clearest way into the Universe is through a forest wilderness."

"One learns that the world, though made, is yet being made. That this is still the morning of creation."

"Nothing goes unrecorded. Every word of leaf and snowflake and particle of dew ... as well as earthquake and avalanche, is written down in Nature's book."

"When we try to pick out anything by itself, we find it hitched to everything else in the universe."

"Reading these grand mountain manuscripts displayed through every vicissitude of heat and cold, calm and storm, up heaving volcanoes and down-grinding glaciers, we see that everything in Nature called destruction must be creation – a change from beauty to beauty."
The drama of the real experience cannot match reading about it or seeing pictures.

"Then it seemed to me the Sierra should be called, not the Nevada, or Snowy Ridge, but the *Range of Light*."

"These beautiful days must enrich all my life. They do not exist as mere pictures . . . but they saturate themselves into every part of the body and live always."

"I have a low opinion of books; they are but piles of stone set up to show coming travelers where other minds have been, or at least signal smokes to call attention ... No amount of word making will ever make a single soul to know these mountains."

Nature is a good mother for nourishment and healing.

"In God's wilderness lies the hope of the world – the great fresh unblighted, unredeemed wilderness. The galling harness of civilization drops off, and the wounds heal ere we are aware."

"Camp out among the grass and gentians of glacier meadows, in craggy garden nooks full of Nature's darlings. Climb the mountains and get their good tidings. Nature's peace will flow into you as sunshine flows into trees. The winds will below their own freshness into you, and the storms their energy, while cares will drop off like autumn leaves."

"Earth has no sorrow that earth cannot heal."

"Nature is a good mother, and sees well to the clothing of her many bairns—birds with smoothly imbricate feathers, beetles with shining jackets, and bears with shaggy furs."

"Everyone needs beauty as well as bread places to play in and pray in, where nature may heal and give strength to body and soul alike."

Human caused destruction of natural areas.
"That anyone would try to destroy such a place seems incredible; but sad experience show that there are people good enough and bad enough for anything." (referring to building Hetch Hetchy reservoir)

"I often wonder what man will do with the mountains—that is, with their utilizable, destructible garments. Will he cut down all the trees to make ships and houses? If so, what will be the final and far upshot? Will human destructions like those of Nature—fire and flood and avalanche—work out a higher good, a finer beauty? … What is the human part of the mountains' destiny?"

Nature is an everlasting chain.
"I only went out for a walk and finally concluded to stay out till sundown, for going out, I found, was really going in."

"This grand show is eternal. It is always sunrise somewhere; the dew is never all dried at once; a show is forever falling; vapor is ever rising. Eternal sunrise, eternal sunset, eternal dawn and gloaming on sea and continents and islands, each in its turn, so the round earth rolls."

Our Stories & Storytelling

John Muir was a gifted storyteller and writer. His ability to be persuasive in his writing was the key to making positive change. Hundreds, if not thousands, of people around the world tell stories. Stories can come from personal experience or combine real life experiences with things that could happen but never really did. Stories can come from faraway lands or instances that occurred long, long ago. Stories contain pieces of information that weave itself together.

Some of the best stories grow as you tell them. The storyteller adds details to make the story come alive right before your eyes, even if it happened last year or 1,000 years ago.

This section is for you to learn how to gather information and create stories – stories about you, your family, your community and people from other places and times.

Stories have been used in different cultures to teach, create change, entertain and pass on family traditions and wisdom for hundreds and thousands of years. Anyone can tell a story and everyone has stories to tell.

Building Storytelling Skills

What makes a good story?"
- ✓ Interesting and believable characters are very important. Sometimes the characters may remind you of yourself or someone you know.
- ✓ Details that make the story come alive. Listeners create images in their imagination. The more details you give, the closer their imagination will match yours. Without the details, listeners make up what they do not know.
- ✓ Every story has a problem or challenge to solve. Someone usually gets into trouble and needs help.
- ✓ Decide if your story will be funny, suspense, adventure or fantasy.

You can use this page to do some brainstorming for story ideas. The *Storytelling Decision Map* on the next page will be a great tool to get you started. When you do interviews of family members or friends, you can use this map to help you "map" how you want to tell their stories.

Inspired by John Muir 39

STORYTELLING DECISION MAP

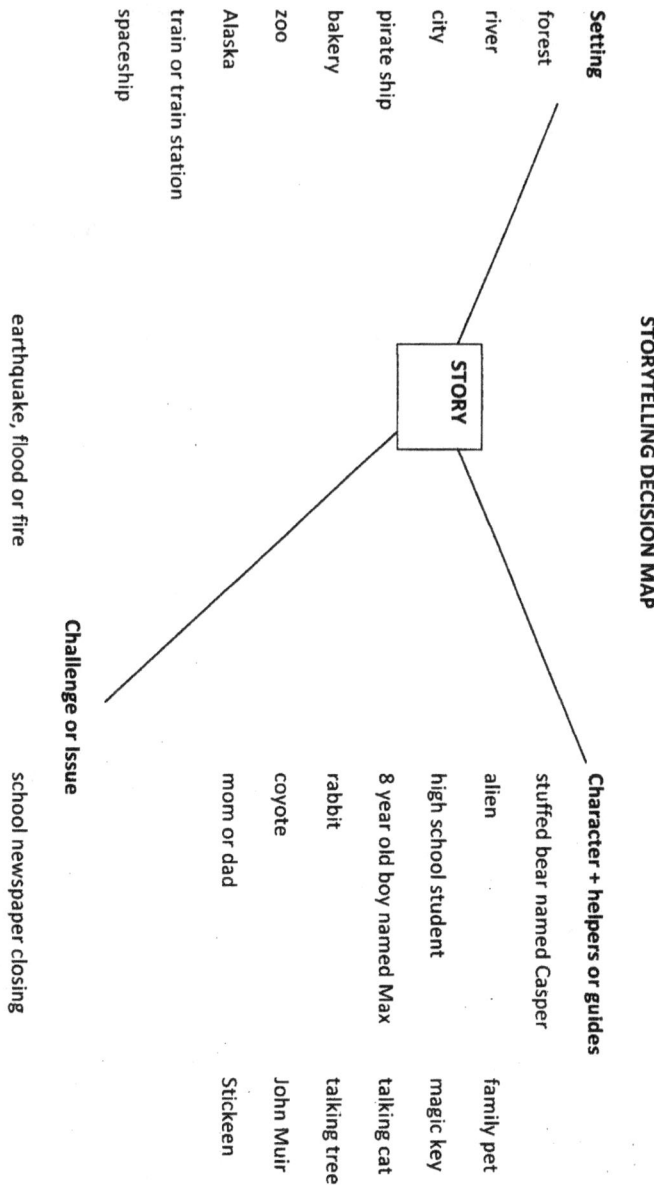

Setting
- forest
- river
- city
- pirate ship
- bakery
- zoo
- Alaska
- train or train station
- spaceship

Character + helpers or guides
- stuffed bear named Casper
- alien — family pet
- high school student — magic key
- 8 year old boy named Max — talking cat
- rabbit — talking tree
- coyote — John Muir
- mom or dad — Stickeen

Challenge or Issue
- school newspaper closing
- friend moves away
- earthquake, flood or fire
- polluted river / no clean water
- parent dies or parents divorce
- mother sends child into the forest with no food

Who Am I?

John Muir's father was a significant influence on how Muir spent his childhood and the man he would become. The values, interests, expertise and cultural traditions of parents and grandparents often play a large role in shaping a child's thoughts about his or her place in the world.

This question asks to tell your stories. Most people have at least one moment or experience in their life they consider memorable or significant. Sometimes, we may not understand the influence of that event at the time. Do you have a memory to write about from this list or add your own? Maybe your have photos to help you remember?

- ✓ Bringing home your first pet
- ✓ Going on a special vacation or visiting a theme park
- ✓ Celebrating a birthday
- ✓ Getting a new pair of shoes
- ✓ When you laughed a lot with your friends about something funny.
- ✓ Imagine a special day when you meet a favorite athlete or celebrity, or visit a place of your dreams.

Family Stories – Past and Present

You may or may not realize how much your family history, culture and background influences food choices, day to day activities, birthday or holiday celebrations or the places you visit. Find out more about your family traditions by asking questions to develop your family's story.
Ask your family if you can get copies of photographs, or important objects in their lives. These items will add important details to your story or stories.

Once you have interviewed your family, ask your friends about their family activities. Notice what is the same and what is different.

Family History Details

Interview one or more parents, grandparents, uncles or aunts and write a story about what you discovered. Remember to refer to the *Storytelling Decision Map* if you need help to create the story.

Family History Interview Questions
- ✓ When did my families arrive in the area?
- ✓ What is the birthplace of my parents or grandparents?
- ✓ How did my parents or grandparents meet? Were there traditions concerning courtship?
- ✓ What work did my grandparents do? What was their mode of transportation?
- ✓ Did they live in the city, country or farm?
- ✓ What games did my parents or elder family members play? What did grandparents do for entertainment? Did they have leisure time?
- ✓ Where did elder family members go to school? What was their highest level of education? What challenges did they face getting an education?
- ✓ What work did my parents do earlier in their life? Did their work change after I was born?
- ✓ What were their favorite foods?
- ✓ Did they have toys?
- ✓ What work did they do?

Other People, Other Places

Like John Muir, people have come to live in America from other places around the world. When families come, they bring their culture and family traditions with them. America has become what is called, a "melting pot" of many nations and cultures all living together.

People from other lands have different stories to share than the ones we know in America. So people bring their stories here too. Their stories help us experience the values, traditions and stories of other cultures beyond what is practiced in your home.

Similar to creating a family history, this project involves interviewing people from a different culture in your neighborhood. Check your community's senior center or local church that represents another culture, if you need help finding people of other cultures.

Other People, Other Places
Suggested Interview Questions

- ✓ Do you have a favorite story from childhood you want to share?
- ✓ What special traditions or holidays did you celebrate in your home country?
- ✓ Does your home country prepare special foods?
- ✓ What toys did you play with? What were some of your favorite games to play?
- ✓ Was there a public park or square you could visit? Where did your family go to have fun?
- ✓ What work did your parents do?
- ✓ What kinds of things did you do with your parents, grandparents or other members of your family?
- ✓ Did you celebrate your birthday? Or holidays?
- ✓ Did you have a phone in your home? If you did not, how did you talk to people outside of your home?
- ✓ Describe the home you lived in. How many rooms? Did it have an indoor kitchen? Did it have bathrooms? Did you have a yard or a garden?
- ✓ How did you go places? Did your family have a car or ride a train?
- ✓ Were there books in your house? What did you read? Was there a library or a bookstore near where you lived?

Our Changing Community

This project involves taking a close look at your neighborhood. You will be looking for places that have changed in the last 100 years and what those places looked like 100 years ago.

Take photos of places, houses and buildings, parks and open space or people that mean something to you. Write the address, name of the place or person, or a one-sentence description of the place you photograph. To find out about the history of the site, you can find a lot of information at your local library.

Write Photo Ideas or other details here

Wonders of Nature

This section creates opportunities to study nature – listen – journal and create a more meaningful connection to the outdoor world. John Muir inspired people to visit and preserve wild places with his detailed descriptions of what he saw and experienced, He came to understand how our lives are all connected to weather, wildlife, plants, forests and landscapes.

Muir looked at and learned from everything with delight – *a rainstorm, a squirrel's chatter, a flower blooming for the first time or sunlight shining on the side of the mountain.* Read the two paragraphs below reprinted from *My First Summer in the Sierra* by John Muir. Notice the words he uses to describe his experiences of the day.

"July 20. Fine calm morning; air tense and clear; not the slightest breeze astir; everything shining, the rocks with wet crystals, the plants with dew, each receiving its portion of irised dewdrops and sunshine like living creatures getting their breakfast…"

"August 10. …After a long ramble through the dense woods I emerged upon a smooth meadow full of sunshine like a lake of light, about a mile and a half long, a quarter to half a mile wide, and bounded by tall arrowy pines.

Muir also noticed changes over a period of time. Noticing changes is one of the **most important** things you can do when studying nature! We need to be observant, so we have evidence to prove when our climate is changing, our trees are diseased, and coyotes, bears, deer, salmon or any other wildlife are disappearing. When we know something has changed, we can take action to begin to solve the problem.

Naturalist Skills

Safety
- ☐ Water - Stay Hydrated
- ☐ Shelter - Clothing
- ☐ Food - What to eat
- ☐ Awareness of harmful plants & animals
- ☐ Other

Observation
- ☐ Activating all your senses
- ☐ Sitting quietly
- ☐ Using a hand lens
- ☐ Other

Identification
- ☐ Using a Field Guide
- ☐ Animals
- ☐ Plants
- ☐ Rock types
- ☐ Scat/Tracks
- ☐ Weather
- ☐ Other

Mapping
- ☐ Identifying directions (North, East, South, West)
- ☐ Making a Map
- ☐ Reading a Map

Documentation
- ☐ Recording Data
- ☐ Journaling
- ☐ Illustration
- ☐ Other

Measurement
- ☐ Tracks/Scat
- ☐ Trees - Width & Height
- ☐ Water temp & clarity
- ☐ Weather - temperature
- ☐ Other

Discovery Journal

Discovery Journals are your "gateway" to observe the natural world up close and personal. These can be your private spaces to write your observations, questions, draw, create art, and record evidence to preserve the memory of your experiences. Or you can choose to share notes when you go outdoors with friends or family.

Types of Journals

All journals are different and serve different purposes. Your journal will be different if you want to keep one journal for each topic you study, one journal for everything, or use a folder to collect objects, or insert loose sheets of information inside. Some suggestions to consider:

Purchase
- ✓ Bound journal of any size (lined or blank)
- ✓ Spiral or perfect bound notebook
- ✓ Ring binder with blank or lined paper and pocket folders
- ✓ Two-pocket folder to hold both loose and bound sheets and objects
- ✓ Accordion pocket folder to hold loose and bound sheets with a flap so nothing falls out

Handmade
- ✓ Standard blank white copy paper and colored cardstock paper covers bound with ribbon inserted through 2 or 3 holes punched in the side or stapled

Other Supplies
- ✓ Writing pencils
- ✓ Colored pencils
- ✓ Sharpie markers

Sample Journal Page for Basic Information

Date: <u>July 5, 2020</u>   **Time**: <u>8:30 am</u>   **Temperature**: <u>65 degrees</u>

Setting: <u>Main Street Park</u>   **Weather**: <u>Cloudy and cool</u>

  What do I see? Feel? Hear? Smell? Begin with a description of the morning sounds, the cool air you feel on your skin, shapes of the clouds, and if there are birds, squirrels or other wildlife roaming around.

  Describe one object at a time, (such as a tree, flower, or insect). What is the size, texture, color and shape? What does the object remind you of? *"The tree stump looks like a baby bear's head… The bark looks like it has two eyes staring at me."*

Draw a picture of one or more objects that you described.

Journal Questions

1. Describe what you see with as much detail as possible.
- ☐ What am I looking at?
- ☐ What is it doing?
- ☐ How does it move, sound, smell, feel (or taste?)
- ☐ What is it shape, color and texture?
- ☐ How BIG or small is it?
- ☐ Other ideas

2. Think about Connections
- ☐ Why is this animal or object here?
- ☐ Where else have I seen this?
- ☐ What else lives nearby?
- ☐ How did this come to live in this place?
- ☐ What does it remind me of?
- ☐ Other ideas

3. Consider the BIG picture
- ☐ What can I learn from it?
- ☐ How does it relate to my school and neighborhood?
- ☐ What more do I want to learn about this?
- ☐ Other ideas

Modified from *The Nature Connection, An Outdoor Workbook for Kids, Families and Classrooms*

Searching for Evidence

See how many items you can find. Mark the items you find and write what you found alongside.

- ☐ Something with a hole
- ☐ Something you can see through
- ☐ Number
- ☐ Letter
- ☐ Something left by animal
- ☐ Feather
- ☐ Something that is rough
- ☐ Something in your favorite color
- ☐ Something that can be crumbled
- ☐ Something with spots
- ☐ Seed pods
- ☐ Something planted
- ☐ Part of a tree
- ☐ **Something curved**
- ☐ Green shoots of plants and flowers
- ☐ Birds singing (heard or seen)
- ☐ Running or dripping water
- ☐ Earthworms or evidence of in dirt
- ☐ Lady bugs or butterflies
- ☐ Scent of damp earth
- ☐ Mud
- ☐ Warm breeze
- ☐ Warm sun
- ☐ Buzzing insects
- ☐ **Swelled buds**

Listen Deeply, Watch Closely

As you read John Muir's description from *My First Summer in the Sierra*, on the Nature Study page, the act of *listen deeply and watch closely*, gives you "new eyes" to describe your outdoor experience. Like learning any new skill, the more time you have to practice, the better you become. Some people have natural talents so the time to improve skills is less. Everyone is different. *One thing is always the same. We can all get better with practice, no matter where we start.*

Take time outdoors to listen deeply and watch closely. In your front or backyard, at the park, at your school or other outdoor space in your neighborhood. What can you see, hear and smell in a garden? Do you see buzzing bees, ladybugs traveling across a leaf, brightly colored flowers, the sweet scent of jasmine or lavender?

Choose a "green space" that you enjoy. Lie on your back and close your eyes. Each time you hear a sound, listen quietly for a moment to identify the sound and raise your thumb into the air. Listen a few more seconds and put your thumb down. Hear another sound, raise your thumb again and repeat for about five minutes or until you don't hear any sounds at all.

When you sit up, write details of what you heard in your journal. You can visit the same place every day or a few times a week to notice if the sounds and sights are the same or if they have changed.

**Remember how important it is to notice changes over time, so you can bring attention to them. The change itself may be a problem that needs to be solved! Fewer fish in the river, cloudy water from pollution or evidence of disease in trees are all examples of how a setting or habitat can change.

"These beautiful days must enrich all my life. They do not exist as mere pictures . . . but they saturate themselves into every part of the body and live always."

Habitat High Rise

This simple activity asks you to look carefully where you are in four different ways. This is called "Habitat High Rise" because you are looking at different habitats as they rise above the ground and into the sky. Different creatures live at different heights. Grass usually grows in the ground. Most plants grow only so high before they spread out instead of growing taller. Birds can live on the ground or in trees. Lizards can climb anywhere. Spiders can spin a web just about anywhere. Mature trees grow high around your head.

Look at everything around you and see what you can find in your Habitat High Rise. Draw a picture of what you see and label the picture.

- ✓ What lies on the ground at your feet?
- ✓ What is at your knees?
- ✓ What is at your shoulders?
- ✓ What is over your head?

Meet a Tree - Trees as Habitat for Life

Examine the tree bark, its branches, leaf canopy and structure. Challenge yourself to guess its age and look for any evidence of disease or holes made by insects or birds in the tree. Questions below are guides to help "meet the tree" and create an understanding of its life and habitat.

Meet a Tree Study Questions

- ✓ How does the tree receive and transport its nutrients to survive?

- ✓ Describe the tree bark. (use descriptive words such as density, texture, scent or color)

- ✓ Where is the tree located? If it lived somewhere else, how would it need to adapt to survive?

- ✓ Draw a leaf or needles from your tree. Look the needles and see if they arranged in a pattern. Are there lines (veins) in the leaf?

- ✓ What the role of the leaves or needles in supporting the life of the tree?

- ✓ Compare the difference between the shape of your body and trees. Are your arms like branches? Do you have a trunk? How do you and the tree receive and transport nutrients through your "trunks?"

- ✓ How do you think this tree reproduces itself?

- ✓ Name three ways or living things that can harm this tree. (not including cut down by a saw)

- ✓ What evidence of other life – past and present do you see? (Woodpecker holes, nest, disease from bark beetles?)

- ✓ Visit a second tree that has different characteristics. Compare the bark, tree canopy, leaves or needles and cones.

Explore a Special Place

Your goal is to monitor activity in a marked area from week to week. This needs to be a space that will remain undisturbed by people, so you can observe what naturally happens. Consider your front or backyard, or a hidden spot at your local park.

Supplies
- 1 roll of duck tape
- Retractable tape measure
- Discovery Journal

Get Started

Measure and mark off a one-foot square area with tape. During the next few days and weeks, return to this place to discover what creatures live here and what activity has happened. Spaces can be marked on the side of a tree. They do not need to be on flat ground.

- Look for certain objects or animals, such as ants crawling on a flower, or a trail left by a snail, or differences in soil color or texture. Is the area stay or dry out easily?
- Have leaves fallen from trees? Is so, what trees? Did the wind blow leaves from a distance? If so, how far?

Bring your Discovery Journal with you each time to draw the site, record your evidence, describe what you observe and how that differs from your previous visit.

What am I?

Clues game one
I am a carnivore and love to eat creatures when they are still living.
My mother lays thousands of eggs in the water.
During the cold winter I like to stay warm, so I hibernate.
I use my long, sticky tongue to catch my food.
My family likes to jump. We can jump up to 20 times the length of our body at one time.
Do not believe it when someone tells you, I will give you warts.

Clues game two
I can smell and hear very well. My eyesight is not as good.
I have a short tail.
My mother and I are both great climbers. We often climb trees.
My diet includes small mammals, insects, grasses, fruits, nuts, berries and sometimes garbage (or a camper's food that is not stored properly)
My color is dark and my mother is very big! She can weigh as much as 500 pounds.

Clues game three
I get very cold in winter. Sometimes I freeze because I cannot wear a coat.
I grow when it rains.
Farmers like me because I nourish their crops.
When I am big, I can be really good at hiding things, so some people use me as a place to dump their trash. That makes me very unhappy.
When I am very big, I can run across an entire state. When I am very small, you may not be able to see me.
People and fish love to swim in me. That makes me happy.

Clues game four
I am the fastest growing of my kind in the world and the widest.
My family has survived for 2,000 or 3,000 years and some even longer.
My seeds are very tiny.
The tallest one of me is 311 feet tall.
We are usually called Giants.

You can find a lot of my family growing in Sequoia National Park.

Clues game five
Most of the time I live in a forest, but I can also live in your backyard.
I am brown with sharp points.
Native Americans have used me for food and medicine.
Squirrels and woodpeckers like to eat me too.
When I am full grown, I vary in size from two inches to twenty-four inches.
The seeds inside of me release when there is a fire to fall to the ground and grow new trees.

Clues Game Six
I am covered with scales and each one is a single color.
My life is short. My siblings live only four days to eleven months.
I am one of 728 species in the United States.
My family is found and flies all over the world.
My life is filled with many changes.
I am small enough to fit in the palm of your hand. But you need a net to catch me.
I sip nectar from flowers through my tongue and pollinate plants.

Clues game seven
I am a mammal.
I am either brown or gray.
I live either in a tree or on the ground all over the world in forests, parks or your backyard. You may have heard me arguing. I can be very noisy.
My teeth never stop growing. No matter how much I chew they never wear down.
My family's favorite foods are nuts, seeds, insects, caterpillars, berries or bark.

Clues game eight
Some people think of me as a good luck charm
There are 5,000 species of me in the world
Poems and stories have been written about me describing me as a grouch and that my house is on fire. All of these ideas are simply not true.
My favorite food is aphids and other insects that eat plants. I have a very big appetite. I get so hungry that I eat 5,000 aphids during my life.

My color may look pretty to you, but it warns predators to "Go away. I taste terrible."
Unfortunately, frogs, spiders and dragonflies often eat my family.
I have seven black spots and a shiny red, round body.

Clues game ten
When I live in the ocean, I am a beautiful silver color.
I live in both fresh water and seawater. That means I am Anadromous.
Fish, seals and bears catch my family. Fishermen catch us in nets.
I weigh about 25 pounds. Some of my family has lived a long time and grown very big. I know some of us have weighed more than 100 pounds.
I lay my eggs in fresh water when I am between 2 to 4 years old and then I die. Most of us never make it back to our home water to spawn.
I have many names. I am called Chinook, King, Coho or Alaskan.

Clues game eleven
I am the largest rodent in North America.
I am a herbivore. My favorite foods are bark, twigs, roots and aquatic plants.
The house I build for my family underwater keeps us safe during the winter from predators.
People call me "nature's engineer" because of my great building skills.
My teeth are so strong that I can chew right through a log.
I change the course of rivers when I build a dam.

Clues game twelve
My feathers are black, red, white and yellow.
I can live as long as 11 years.
My tongue has sharp points to help me catch worms. I like to grab the side of trees and search for worms.
Some people think I am very noisy and do not appreciate my music.
You may have heard my song on a tree, a utility pole, a trashcan or your chimney.
People usually call my music pecking. My family calls it drumming in rhythm.

Advocacy

John Muir was an advocate for wild lands and wildlife. Advocacy can be any action you want to see changed for the better. One example is wanting your local park, state or national parks to stay beautiful and wild, instead of being spoiled by things that cause air or water pollution or harm wildlife

"I often wonder what man will do with the mountains—that is, with their utilizable, destructible garments. Will he cut down all the trees to make ships and houses? If so, what will be the final and far upshot? Will human destructions like those of Nature—fire and flood and avalanche—work out a higher good, a finer beauty? ... What is the human part of the mountains' destiny?"

Meet a Modern Day John Muir

Research

Activist (volunteer leader of local environmental organization)
Arborist
Biologist
Botanist
Ecologist
Environmental educator
Field researcher
Geologist
Horticulturalist
Lobbyist
Master Gardener
Naturalist
Park Ranger
Rancher / Farmer
Sierra Club staff member
Urban Forester

Create a poster

Learn more about the work involved in the careers listed above by researching specific career descriptions, education and skills. All of them apply similar skills and practices to those that John Muir applied during his lifetime.

- ✓ Title your poster with the name of the profession you researched, such as *"What does a Botanist do?"*
- ✓ Describe in a list or as sentences what the job is, his or her education and skills.
- ✓ Use both *primary* and *secondary* sources, such as the Internet, parents, school books, materials found in the public library or the workplaces where the professional holds his job.
- ✓ Use descriptive words, stories, illustrations, photographs or other materials, to create your poster. Be creative and add three-dimensional items to your poster, as available.
- ✓ Posters can also compare the profession today to that of John Muir's day. For example, *"Careers in Botany: 100 years ago and today."*

    - Primary sources include talking or writing to the person you are researching.
    - Secondary sources include finding information about the person from a newspaper, Internet or book.

Advocacy Project

Use this project to learn about how advocacy works, so you can use the same practices for other issues you read about where you want to get involved. Start by identifying a current environmental or conservation issue or problem. If you do not already know what issue you want to study, ask your parents to help identify some reported in a newspaper, TV news, local magazine, Internet or social media site.

Sample Ideas in Your Neighborhood
- ✓ A city park trail alongside a creek was flooded. Six months later it is not repaired. Hikers have created their own new trail and destroyed the plants next to the creek. Write to the park department asking when the trail will be repaired and report the damage.
- ✓ You want to walk to school safely. There are no sidewalks or marked crosswalks. Contact your city or local nonprofit organization, such as Safe Routes to Schools. Ask how to get involved in finding a solution.

Once you have selected an issue to study, find out if there is an opportunity for you to take action. Research the history of the problem and gather current facts. Check the library, read newspaper articles, magazines or search the Internet to find out more about the issue or problem. Identify what agency or agencies you can contact for information and assistance to resolve the issue.

When finished with your research, write about you discovered about the issue, who else is involved and what you think needs to be done about it. Then get involved where you can to take action.

Role of Resource Agencies

In California, both the federal government and the state government are landowners. They are often considered either "natural or cultural resource agencies" because they manage property with trees, plants, wildlife, rivers (natural) and/or objects (cultural) that need to be protected, such as broken pieces of bones, pottery, grinding stones or grave markers.

The National Park Service owns places such as the John Muir National Historic Site, Muir Woods, Golden Gate National Recreation Area, Yosemite National Park and Sequoia and Kings Canyon National Park. As landowners, they are caretakers of the land, manage the wildlife as needed, and provide services for hikers, campers and other visitors. California State Parks and its related friends groups operate hundreds of parks and monuments across the state. *See preservation and conservation defined in glossary in the back of this book.*

Many other public and private agencies are also landowners. City and county parks are the most visible in your neighborhood. Land trusts, conservancies and other associations also own land so it can be preserved. Some people know very little about the roles and responsibilities of these organizations, so their missions are often misunderstood.

This topic gives you an opportunity to research and learn more bout the people and the agencies that care for wild lands and wildlife in California and across the nation.

Actions
- Conduct research on any of the agencies or organizations listed below to identify the mission and role of the agency and ways they invite the public to be involved.
- Identify at least 3 specific special features and/or wildlife the agency protects.
- Create a poster with text and images to describe the agency's role

Selected Public Agencies
- ✓ Bureau of Land Management
- ✓ Bureau of Reclamation
- ✓ California Department of Fish and Wildlife (or related agencies in other states)
- ✓ California Department of State Parks and Recreation
- ✓ Individual cities and county parks
- ✓ National Park Service
- ✓ US Department of Fish and Wildlife
- ✓ US Forest Service
- ✓ US Army Corps of Engineers
- ✓ Sierra Nevada Conservancy
- ✓ Coastal Conservancy, State of California
- ✓ Sacramento-San Joaquin Delta Conservancy

Selected Nonprofit / Private Organizations
- ✓ Rails to Trails Conservancy
- ✓ John Muir Land Trust
- ✓ Save the Redwoods League
- ✓ The Nature Conservancy

For a more complete list of land trusts and conservancies located in California, see *California Council of Land Trusts*.

My Vision for the Future

Write out your vision for the future of your community or the earth in a few sentences. When you are done, you can use keywords from your vision on a bookmark or any of the suggestions listed below.

Suggestions for Personal Slogans

- ✓ Be a friend to the earth!
- ✓ Keep exploring!
- ✓ Ask questions and wonder.
- ✓ Step lightly.
- ✓ Live simple.
- ✓ Care for the environment.
- ✓ Plant a tree (or a seed).
- ✓ Live by example.
- ✓ Take Action!
- ✓ Clean a place that is dirty.
- ✓ Share your passion for the earth with those you love.
- ✓ Make your own discoveries
- ✓ Go into the wilderness.

Supplies

- 8 1/2 x 11 sheets of heavy weight white paper, index card stock or construction paper
- Ribbon, yarn, other decorative art supplies and white or gel glue
- Single-hole punch
- Markers or colored pencils

Instructions

- Write your personal slogan on a bookmark and decorate it by drawing a picture, or by gluing on ribbons or other art supplies.
- Use one sheet of paper to make four bookmarks.
- Fold paper in half across the short side and then in half again.
- Unfold the paper and cut on the fold lines.
- Write your name and personal slogan on one or both sides before decorating the bookmark.
- Cut a strip of ribbon to about 9" in length
- Use a one hole punch to punch a hole in the top of the bookmark
- Thread the ribbon through the hole and tie the ribbon into a double knot, so the knot is tied tightly.

Cut on all three dotted lines

Part Three

Appendix

Story of John Muir: Answer Sheet

	Key Words	
respect	wandered	observe
treasured	active	exploring
ancient	magnificent	ability
examine	struggle	defend
ambition	reverse	triumph
solutions	surveyed	globe
ordeal	opponents	outcome
individuals	journey	solutions

John Muir learned to love and (**respect**) nature when he was a young boy at his family's farm in Scotland. He (**wandered**) through fields and forests to (**observe**) the birds, squirrels and other wildlife. Muir always (**treasured**) nature. "Climb the mountains and get their good tidings. Nature's peace will flow into you as sunshine flows into the trees."

Muir also had an (**active**) imagination and a lot of (**ambition**) that led to his becoming an inventor. However, Muir could not separate himself from (**exploring**) nature for long. He set out on a (**journey**) of 1,000 miles.

A few years later, Muir lived and worked in Yosemite Valley, among the (**magnificent**) and (**ancient**) redwood trees. He took many risks to (**examine**) the rocks in Yosemite to gather scientific evidence that glaciers carved the valley. Muir also climbed trees in wind and rainstorms to discover how they behaved.

For more than 25 years, Muir (**struggled**) to (**defend**) the forest and wilderness areas. He had the (**ability**) to write persuasive articles so (**individuals**) would be interested in finding (**solutions**) to preserve wilderness for future generations to enjoy. He worked hard to (**reverse**) the damage to forests and habitats as the (**outcome**) of too much logging.

One of his many (**triumphs**) was influencing President Roosevelt to create five national parks. Muir (**surveyed**) forests around the (**globe**) to help preserve them. Muir's last battle was to prevent the construction of a dam in the Hetch Hetchy Valley. The (**ordeal**) lasted 10 years and in the end, his (**opponents**) won.

John Muir Biography Questions Answer Sheet

What was one of John Muir's first encounters with nature as a young boy?
He was with his brother searching tide pools for crabs and other interesting creatures of the sea near his childhood home in Scotland. He climbed the walls of the ruins of Dunbar Castle. Muir regularly visited the shore and the meadows where he could study the creatures and wildlife living there.

Describe at least one of John Muir's inventions.
Study desk
Sawmill was used in a stream to cut wood
Barometers

What was the reason he went on his 1,000-mile walk to the Gulf of Mexico? Describe one or more of the experiences he shared about his journey.
John Muir knew he could not work in a factory again because there was so much to explore and learn about the outdoors. For the first time in his life, he saw tall trees and dense forests. He saw high mountains and deep valleys. Muir took note of flowering plants. There were kind families that offered him food and shelter.

What did he discover about how Yosemite was formed?
Glaciers had cut their way through the rocks to carve the Yosemite Valley. He measured the height and width of rocks and boulders as evidence. Many people disagreed with him at the time, although later he was proven to be right.

What else did John Muir do in Yosemite Valley?
John Muir was a nature guide, leading visitors to his favorite scenic spots. As a guide, he pointed out the evidence of rocks carved by glaciers in several locations. He was also a shepherd. He also met President Roosevelt to camp in Yosemite to convince him how important it was to establish Yosemite as a national park for the public good.

Why did John Muir live on a ranch?

John Muir married John Strentzel's daughter. Strentzel owned a large fruit ranch in Martinez, CA. When Muir married Louise, they lived on the ranch and raised their family. John managed the ranch after his father-in-law died.

What motivated John Muir to spend his life protecting wild lands?

He believed that the wonders of nature in America should be preserved as national parks for generations of people to visit and enjoy. He loved the wilderness and finding out more about nature. When Muir saw indications that man was destroying natural areas, he decided to share his experiences with others by writing articles and books.

Did John Muir act alone or did he have support to make changes happen? If so, name two people who supported him?

No, John Muir did not act alone most of the time. He had support from Ezra and Janine Carr, John Swett and Teddy Roosevelt. Muir helped to form the Sierra Club. By working together, Congress passed laws that protected the wilderness and created national parks for people to enjoy, instead of being destroyed by logging.

List some of the topics that Muir wrote about.

Glaciers	Trips to Alaska
His first summer in the Sierra	Stickeen
Saving wilderness	Preserving Yosemite
Mountains of California	

Who Was John Muir?

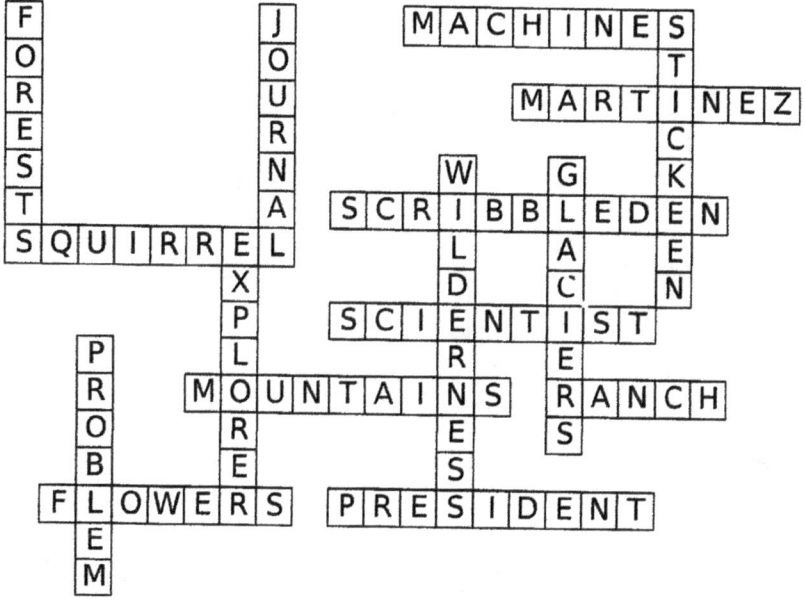

John Muir: The Scientist

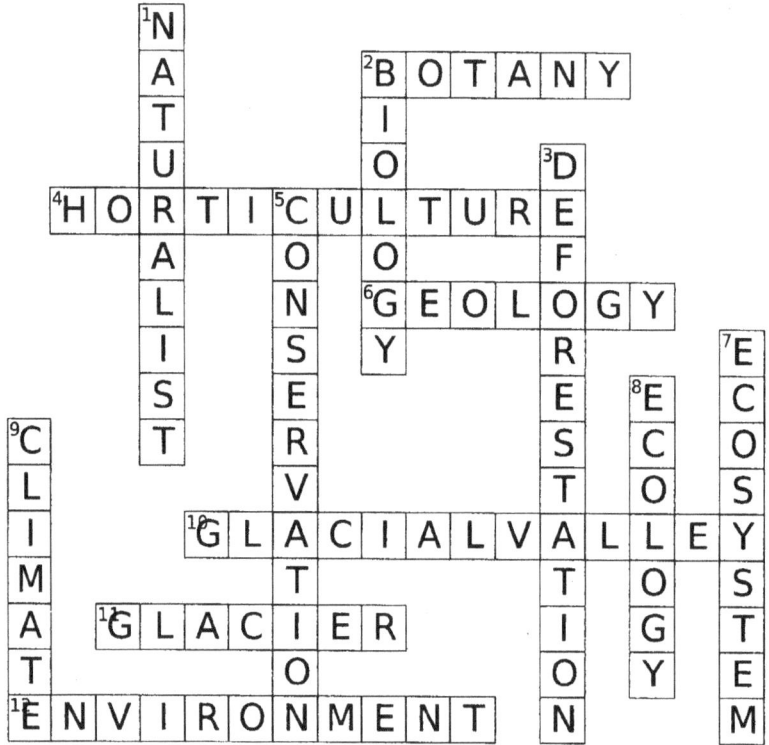

What Am I? Answers

Clue One	frog
Clue Two	bear
Clue Three	river
Clue Four	Redwood trees
Clue Five	pinecones
Clue Six	butterfly
Club Seven	squirrel
Clue Eight	snake
Clue Nine	ladybug
Clue Ten	salmon
Clue Eleven	beaver
Clue Twelve	woodpecker

Books About John Muir

Dunham, Montrew. (1998). *John Muir, Young Naturalist.* Aladdin Paper backs: New York, NY.

Dunlap, Julie. (2004). John Muir and Stickeen: An icy adventure with a no good dog. Northword Press: Chanhassen, MN.

Faber, Doris. (1991). *Nature and the environment: Great Lives.* Charles Scribner's Sons: New York, NY.

Lasky, K. (2006). *John Muir: America's first environmentalist.* Candlewick Press: Cambridge, MA.

Mcully, E. A. (2003). *Squirrel and John Muir.* First ed. New York, NY: Farrar Straus Giroux. (suitable for younger readers)

Muir, J. (1998). *John Muir and the brave little dog.* Dawn Publications: Nevada City, CA.

Wadsworth, G. (1992). *John Muir, Wilderness Protector.* Lerner Publications: Minneapolis, MN.

Wadsworth, G. (2009). *Camping with the president.* Calkins Creek: Honesdale, PA.

Warrick, K. C. (2002). John Muir: Crusader for the wilderness. Enslow Publisher: Berkeley Heights, NJ.

Glossary

Biodegradable. When an object can be decomposed either by living organisms or naturally over time back into the earth.

Biology. The branch of science that deals with the origin, history, physical characteristics, life processes and habits of living organisms.

Botany. The branch of science that studies plants, life cycle, structure, growth and classification.

Climate. Weather patterns of a particular place that occur over a period of years, such as cloudiness, temperature, air pressure, humidity, rainfall and winds.

Conservation. A complex term that addresses the careful use of natural resources to prevent injury, waste, decay or loss. Also refers to the official supervision of rivers, forests, and other natural resources in order to preserve and protect them through prudent management.

Deforestation. Cutting down (or clearing) massive amounts of trees so quickly, the forest has no time to grow back. This action often results in damage to the quality of the land.

Ecology. The branch of science that examines the relationships that organisms have to each other and to their environment. Scientists who study those relationships are called ecologists.

Ecosystem. A geographic area where plants, animals, and other organisms, as well as weather and landscape, work together and depend on each other to sustain life.

Environment. The physical world we live in, including all the circumstances that surround and influence life on earth, the atmosphere, food chain and water cycle.

Garden. The area immediately surrounding the Muir House, where trees, shrubs and flowers are planted. This is separate from the ranch used for agriculture.

Geology. The area of science that deals with the dynamics, physical history and structure of the earth; including the rocks and rock formations, and the physical, chemical, and biological changes that have occurred and continue to occur.

Glacial Moraine. A mass of loose rock, soil, and earth that sits in front of a glacier as it moves down a drainage or valley and then deposited by the edge of a glacier when movement has stopped. A terminal moraine marks the location where the glacier stopped.

Glacial Valley. A steep-sided, U-shaped valley formed by erosion when glaciers move through a drainage or river channel.

Glacier. An extended mass of ice formed from snow falling and accumulating where the rate of snowfall exceeds the rate at which snow melts. The ice moves very slowly, either descending from high mountains, as in valley glaciers, or moving outward from centers of accumulation, as in continental glaciers

Hetch Hetchy. Name of the reservoir formed when a dam was built that flooded the Hetch Hetchy Valley. The existence of the dam to this day remains controversial. The Restore Hetch Hetchy group continues its fervent advocacy efforts in favor of its restoration. The dam is located within the boundary of Yosemite National Park and provides water for San Francisco residents and businesses.

Horticulture: The art or science of growing flowers, fruits, vegetables and shrubs in gardens or orchards.

Mt. Wanda and Mt. Helen. Mountain tops that John Muir named after his daughters.

Muir Glacier. A glacier located in Southeast Alaska, in the St. Elias Mountains, flowing southeast from Mount Fairweather. Covers about 350 square miles.

Natural history. The sciences, such as botany, mineralogy, or zoology, concerned with the study of all subjects in the natural world.

Naturalist. A person who either studies, or is an expert in, nature or natural history as a result of direct observation of animals or plants.

Preservation: To keep safe from harm or injury; protect or spare, keep alive.

Bibliography

Clark, J. H. & Sargent, S. (Eds.). (1985). *Dear papa: Letters between John Muir and his daughter Wanda.* Fresno, CA: Panorama West Books.

Douglas, W. O. (1961). *Muir of the mountains.* Boston, MA: Houghton Mifflin Co.

Graves, C. (1973). *John Muir.* New York, NY: Thomas Crowell Company.

Killion, J. (2005). *Cultural Landscape Report for John Muir National Historic Site* (Vol. 1). Boston, MA: National Park Service.

National Park Service. *John Muir National Historic Site.* "Places and things named for John Muir."

Worster, D. (2008). *A passion for nature.* New York, NY: Oxford University Press.

Author Bio

Janice Kelley is an award-winning author and naturalist, passionate about inspiring meaningful connections to people, places, rivers and wildlife. She delights in sharing the wonders and curiosities of the outdoor world with youth and adults during guided walks, interpretive programs, workshops and spoken word stories. She draws inspiration from the life and quotations of John Muir, Aldo Leopold, Joseph Cornell and other environmental champions.

As founder and leader of the *Nature Detectives* program, Janice creates opportunities for children in kindergarten through third grade to discover the outdoor world – online and in person. The program's website https://naturedetectivesusa.com presents a variety of resources for children and parents, with leader training option for teachers and site staff.

Janice describes her own experiences in the outdoor world in blogs and photography on her website, https://naturelegacies.com. "Mornings on Fair Oaks Bridge, Watching Wildlife at the Lower American River," is a 200-page full-color book featuring a selection of 75 of 200 blogs posts on her website.

She completed her Master of Science degree in Recreation, Parks and Tourism Administration from California State University, Sacramento, 2013. At graduation, Janice was one of two students to receive the department's annual *Award of Merit*.

www.ingramcontent.com/pod-product-compliance
Lightning Source LLC
Chambersburg PA
CBHW080401030426
42334CB00024B/2954